Learn to Knit the Old Fashioned Way

The Joy of Learning to Knit
Five Simple Projects to Learn to Knit Today

By

Jessica Dorsey

Dear Reader,

This practical knitting guide was written and designed just for you! It is lovingly dedicated to those who have learned to knit throughout the ages... to the countless individuals who have learned the art of knitting and have taken the time to pass this wonderful hobby on to the next generation.

I would like to thank everyone who has shared precious memories about learning to knit with me, and would like to express my appreciation to Microsoft, iCLIPART, and Abram's Photos for the use of the images in this guide.

Please feel free to contact me if you would like more information about this book, or about any of my other books. I look forward to your emails and to hearing about your experiences with knitting!

With gratitude,

Jessica Dorsey

jessicadorsey18@yahoo.com

Learn to Knit the Old Fashioned Way: The Joy of Learning to Knit
Five Simple Projects to Learn to Knit Today
JDorsey©2013

Table of Contents

Why Learn to Knit?

"When I knit, I remember my mother sitting next to me, patiently helping me unravel tangled messes, redoing rows of garter stitch…watching as I learned to wind a skein of yarn into a colorful ball." Julie

Knitting is an art that stretches back over the centuries, passed from mother to daughter over the years. Sadly, today many families are separated by miles and what was once tradition is no longer the rule.

However, with a renewed appreciation for knitting many people want to learn to knit. Yarn colors, textures, and lovely patterns provide countless ways to create unique and special designs that can be worn, given as gifts, and sold!

Knitting is a wonderful activity, a take-along hobby that can add to almost every daily experience in a way that provides beauty, pleasure, and a sense of accomplishment.

This simple guide is designed to give beginning knitters the basic tools they need in order to learn to knit. It is combined with the special memories of several individuals, memories that can be traced back to early experiences in an unbroken chain that was passed from generation to generation. Now you too may join that cherished circle of knitters.

Simply Original: Knitting

"I remember the booties my mother helped me knit for our next door neighbor's new baby, tiny white booties that weren't much bigger than my mother's thumb. We carefully threaded satin ribbon through the eyelets, then shared the joy of presenting the paper-wrapped package to our neighbor for her newly adopted infant." Jane

Once you have learned to knit, you will find it quite easy to add onto the basic skills that are included in this guide. Many women, children, and men have discovered that knitting is a relaxing, pleasurable, and meaningful hobby. In just a few hours you too can learn to knit. By following a few simple steps and becoming familiar with the proper tools, you will find yourself knitting in no time at all! As you practice, you'll be able to improve on these basic skills. Knitting will become easier and much more enjoyable than you could have ever imagined.

The pleasures of knitting are countless. Once you have learned to knit, you'll be able to style hand-knit items that you can wear and enjoy. You'll create gifts that are made with love, and make items that you can sell. Custom knit projects are original and have their own unique qualities. Hand-made clothing and accessories maintain an ageless appeal.

Once you have mastered these few basic techniques you will be able to knit clothing and accessories for every occasion. Clothes can be knit in styles and colors that are custom-made and fashionable. Today, yarn is available in a vast array of rich blends, textures, and shades. Designs can be simple and basic, as well ornate and dramatic!

Knitting is the perfect hobby for everyone who enjoys creating something original. While the basic steps are simple, knitting allows for intricate work. It is a wonderful pastime and a delightful way to prepare for upcoming events like the birth of a baby or the long winter months. Whether you have time on your hands, are traveling, bedridden, or watching a movie, knitting is a hobby that lends itself to most every occasion, night or day.

By following these guidelines, you are ready to begin learning today!

Selecting Yarn and Supplies

"Walking into a yarn shop is like walking into a candy store. The colors seem to jump from the shelves. When I enter the yarn section, I feel like the whole world opens up and the possibilities are beyond measure" Lee

Just as everything you knit has its own style and charm, every type of yarn has its own unique character. Yarns that are made of natural fibers have a fresh, clean, and sporty appearance, while wool and wool-blends tend to be warmer and more versatile. The joy of knitting comes from selecting just the right yarn for that special project.

When you shop for yarn, always check the washing instructions and weight. Today yarn is available in megastores, most stores that carry craft supplies, and online. The many varieties of yarn are designed for particular uses: for items like baby clothes, children's sweaters, winter clothing, and knit-afghans. The beauty is that the choice is yours! The patterns, on pages 34-42, allow you to experiment with new yarn or use what you already have on hand.

Included in this book are simple step-by-step instructions that will help you learn to knit today. At the end of the guide are five very basic projects that you'll be able to knit using the yarn you've selected. It is recommended that beginners start by using a medium weight yarn that won't unravel easily. Medium sized needles are suggested because they tend to be easier for beginning knitters to handle. The following chart shows the US/UK/Metric needle size comparisons.

Knitting Needle Conversion Chart

US Needle Sizes	UK Needle Sizes	Metric Needle Sizes
0	14	2.0mm
1	13	2.25mm
2	12	2.75mm
-	11	3.0mm
3	10	3.25mm
4	-	3.5mm
5	9	3.75mm
6	8	4.0mm
7	7	4.5mm
8	6	5.0mm
9	5	5.5mm
10	4	6.0mm
10 ½	3	6.5mm
-	2	7.0mm
-	1	7.5mm
11	0	8.0mm
13	00	9.0mm
15	000	10.0mm
17	-	12.0mm
19	-	16.0mm
35	-	19.0mm
50	-	25.0mm

When selecting yarn and supplies *the most important rule* is to have fun! Learning to knit requires some effort, so patience does pay off… the more pleasure you take in the materials you use, the more joy you will experience while knitting!

Learning to Knit: 1, 2, 3...

"I learned to knit in the third grade, back in 1941. We were asked to knit squares to be used in blankets for the soldiers. It was a wonderful way to learn, thinking we were doing something for the war effort...I often reassured myself that although my 'square' was lopsided, it could be matched up with another lopsided square to come out even." Carole

Learning to knit is a process that requires a few simple steps. If you learn good habits from the start, you'll continue to improve your skills. It is recommended that you review the steps periodically; soon you will master these basic techniques and will on your way to developing your own knitting style.

1. Learn what the abbreviations mean!

Knitting uses a type of shorthand (abbreviations) in most knitting patterns. These simple abbreviations will direct your steps throughout the instructions. The following chart provides some of the most commonly used abbreviations. In this guide they are written in lower case. Some directions may use capitalized abbreviations or a combination of lower and upper case letters (i.e. K-KNIT or k-Knit).

Commonly Used Knitting Abbreviations

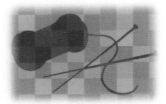

K...knit

p...purl

sl...slip

yo...yarn over

st(s)...stitches

sl st...slip stitch

inc...increase

dec..decrease

tog...together

dp ....double point

psso..pass the slip stitch over a knit stitch

An asterisk (*) tells you when the pattern will be repeated. The instructions following the asterisk need to be repeated the number of times that the pattern specifies.

Work-even means that you will need to knit without making any changes or adjustments. Continue with the pattern the same way that you began.

2. Read through the directions before beginning to knit!

Check over all of the instructions before beginning, making sure that the sequence of instructions makes sense. Then, as you begin the project, follow a step-by-step sequence so you don't skip any steps.

3: Understand the meaning of "gauge".

"The first sweater that I knit seemed ten sizes too large. I quickly learned how important it is to check the gauge!" Candace

The term "gauge" refers to the exact number of knit stitches and knit rows that are required to create a square with a given measurement. Usually gauge is measured in square inches (or square centimeters). Most patterns will follow a specific gauge. If you check the gauge before beginning a pattern you will be more likely to have a correctly sized finished piece.

It is important to check the gauge before you start every new project. This way you can adjust your knitting, if necessary, by using different needles, and/or by decreasing or increasing the number of stitches required per row. Correct needle size and gauge make it more likely that you will be satisfied with the completed project. If gauge is accurately checked and stitch size remains uniform you can avoid unnecessary frustration.

A simple procedure, that helps to determine gauge, is to knit a small square with the yarn. This square is called a "swatch". Once you have knit your swatch, count the number of stitches down and across - included in the square measurement. After you have satisfactorily determined the gauge, you are ready to begin your project.

(The five projects included in this guide are designed to allow for some flexibility with gauge.)

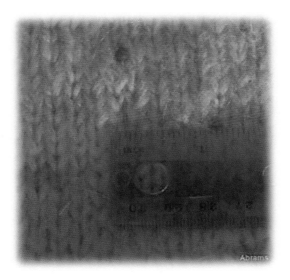

Note - Measure gauge simply by placing two straight pins at a ninety degree angle (an inch apart) on the "swatch" sample and count the stitches between each pin.

4. Finish each row!

"When I was a child we had a cat named Minnie-Mouse-Catcher. Minnie enjoyed my knitting as much as I did. One time she pulled the scarf I was knitting off the needles, and I found her lying in the tangled heap on the floor." Laura

If you put your knitting down before you finish a row, you run the risk of having your stitches stretch and/or slip off the needles. Besides dropping stitches, the gauge may be thrown off and you may forget where you left off. If you find you must put your knitting down, when midway through a row, set the needles down in a place where they are unlikely to be disturbed. Then when you are ready to begin knitting again, carefully pick up the skein (or ball) with your right hand so that you're ready to begin. This is particularly important with respect to gauge.

5. Knit and Purl Combinations

A design is made from two basic types of knitting stitches: the k…knit and the p… purl. The k tells you when you need to knit, and the p will instruct you when to purl. You will continue with the k or p stitch for as long as the instructions indicate.

Most patterns tell you when you will make a change or an adjustment. You will be told when to cast on, knit, purl, increase, decrease, etc. Patterns are designed to show you how to create each project. Below are photographs that show samples of the most common types of knit designs.

The Simple Garter Stitch

"When I taught my daughter to knit we picked out a set of purple needles and bought a large skein of lavender yarn. As we went through the process, we took it a step at a time. In less than a week my daughter had made her first scarf."
Vanessa

A simple garter stitch is the most basic knitting style. This is a great stitch for beginning knitters to learn. A simple garter stitch looks like the swatch in the picture below. It consists of one knit row after another. Both sides of the project will look the same, therefore only one photo is provided in this sample.

The Basic Stockinet Stitch – "Right" Side

When you knit a row and purl a row you will create a basic stockinet stitch. In the two examples below, you can see that both sides have a distinctive appearance.

When the knit pattern looks like this…

…you will know that you just finished a purl row, and you will begin knitting the next row. (The above picture is an example of the "right" side of the stockinet stitch.)

The Basic Stockinet Stitch – "Wrong" Side

"Knitting is a hobby that I share with my daughter. I look forward to the day when she has her own children and we can teach them to knit!" Karyn

If the knitting in your left hand looks like the photo below, you will know that your last row was a knit row and it is again time to purl. (This example also shows the "wrong" side of a stockinet pattern.)

The Basic Rib-Stitch

Ribbing allows for stretching; it is great to use for cuffs and bands. When forming ribs, the pattern will tell you to knit and purl a certain number of stitches across the row (one, two, or more stitches). You will then knit over the knit stitches and purl over the purl stitches. (Below is an example of a basic rib-stitch using k-2, p-2.)

The Seed Stitch

Seed stitch patterns are made up of a knit-purl, knit-purl pattern that alternates on each row. As a general rule, an odd number of stitches across the row will result in a seed pattern, while an even number will result in a ribbed pattern. Your directions will instruct you to knit over a purl stitch and to purl over a knit stitch. (If you knit a k-p combination with an even number of stitches in a row, you will then start the next row with the alternate pattern; for example in row one, k-p-k-p..., row two, p-k-p-k...)

Combination Patterns

"Knitting helps to keep my hands busy when I'm waiting at the dentist or doctor's office." Elizabeth

Many interesting patterns can be created with a combination of knit and purl stitches. The following sample is designed by knitting four rows of seed stitches followed by four rows of stockinet stitches. This is just one example of the interesting patterns that you will be able to create!

Below: The seed stitch was used on the front of this sweater.

Enjoying Knitting: A, B, C...

"It's relaxing to knit while talking with my husband, watching a romantic movie, or while listening to the rain on the rooftop!" Alexandra

Casting-On-

The first step in the knitting process involves casting-on. While there are several methods for casting-on, the following procedure provides a sturdy beginning row for your project. Once you have cast-on the number of stitches that your pattern specifies, you will be ready to start the next row.

After you have cast-on the stitches, your stitches will be on the right-hand needle and you'll be ready to begin your project. When you have finished the next row, the stitches will be transferred to the left-hand needle. You will then switch this needle back into your right hand, to begin the process again. This will hold true whether you are knitting or purling the next stitches. (Note: If you are left-handed, you will be working in the opposite manner.)

The method that is recommended in this book involves knitting-on the stitches. This "base" provides a strong cast-on row. When you cast-on the beginning stitches you will want to pull each new stitch slightly, but not too tightly! If the stitches are pulled too forcefully it will be more difficult to insert the needle when forming the next stitch. This step will become easier as you grow more familiar with the process.

Step A… The following picture demonstrates the way to tie your first slipknot from which you will begin your project (a). You will want to leave a strand of about eight to ten inches.

a

Step B… The ball or skein of yarn will remain on your right side; the tail will then be on your left side. After you make your knot (b), you will pull the strand around that needle and secure the knot.

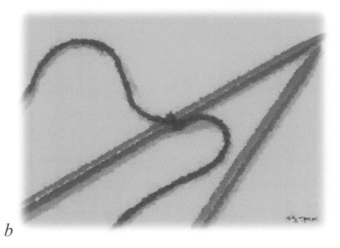

b

Step C… The slip-knot is now completed. In the next picture you can see how the loose end of the yarn is held by the left hand and the skein of yarn is supported by the right hand. The righthand needle will then be slipped beneath the lefthand needle. The strand of yarn that you will be working with (from the skein or the ball) is then supported by your righthand index finger (c).

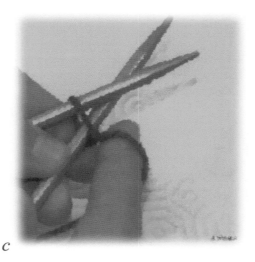

c

Step D… You will now begin to cast-on by drawing the yarn up with your right index fnger, around, and down through the V formed by the two needles (d).

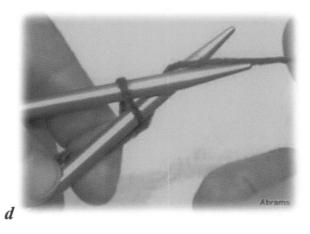

d

Step E… Now manipulate the righthand needle and "catch" the strand of yarn by pulling the loop up, out, and towards you with the point of your righthand needle (e).

e

Step F... Next, continue to gently guide this loop of yarn (using the righthand needle), bring it up, forward, and over the top of the lefthand knitting needle, pulling the stitch around the top of the needle (f); gently tighten the stitch. You have just successfully formed your very first cast-on stitch!

f

Step G... The yarn strand from your skein (or ball) of yarn is still held in your righthand. You will continue the process described above for the next cast-on stitches. Continue to insert your righthand needle-point underneath the lefthand needle, sticking it underneath and through the stitch that was just made. Again, wrap the yarn with your righthand index finger around from behind, and through the "v", catching this loop with the righthand knitting needle and guiding the loop back up, and over the lefthand knitting needle tip by repeating the same upwards-outwards gesture that you used in creating the last cast-on stitch. Once you tighten this new loop, you will have cast-on a new stitch. Continue this procedure until you have successfully cast-on the stitches for your project. The first, slip-knot that you made is considered to be one of the stitches (g).

g

Ready to Knit-

"My first project was a simple headband. I made it when I was in fourth grade. I used yarn that reminded me of a box full of crayons, from a ball of wool that I found in my mother's knitting basket. I remember how proud I was the first time I wore my new headband to school!" Sarah

Once you have cast-on the stitches, you are ready to begin knitting your first project.

Step H… Your cast-on stitches will be in your left hand. Once again, take your right-hand needle and slip it through the first cast-on stitch (at the top of the left-hand needle) just as you did while casting-on. Always slip the needle through the loop, from the front to the back of the needle (h).

h

Step I... Bring the yarn with your right-hand index finger around the back of the right-hand needle up and towards you, through the "v", in the same way that you did when you were casting-on (i).

i

Step J... Continuing to firmly hold the strand of yarn with the right-hand index finger, pull the right needle towards you, bringing the newly formed loop through the first loop on the left-hand needle. Now, slip the new loop off the tip of the left-hand needle onto the tip of the right-hand needle (j). Once you have completed this step, you will have completed your first stitch.

j

Step K…Continue to knit the next stitches. Once you have knit all of the cast-on stitches, your newly knit stitches will on the right-hand needle. Again transfer the right-hand needle (with the stitches) into your left hand. You will again be holding the empty needle in your right hand. At this point, you are again ready to knit (or purl) a new row.

For a garter stitch pattern, you will repeat the rows with knit stitches for the remainder of the rows. For a stockinet pattern, you will knit a row and then purl a row, alternating these two types of stitches as you go (k).

Simple Garter Stitch and Simple Stockinet Stitch

k

Ready to Purl -

Step L…To purl, begin by inserting the right-hand needle in the opposite direction from when you are making a knit-stitch. You will begin by inserting the right-needle through the loop, in front of the left-hand needle, in a downwards direction. Next, you will carry the yarn (supporting it with your right-hand index finger) down, between the V formed by the needles. The picture below shows you how to carry the yarn over and under, continuing around the right-hand needle to form the loop.

l

Step M…Next, with the right-hand needle, bring the newly formed loop through the first stitch on your left-hand needle.

m

Step N…Continue, with your right-hand needle pulling it down - slightly under the tip of the left-hand needle - and off, to create the new stitch. (You'll bring the loop off of the left-hand needle, sliding the newly created stitch onto the needle in your right hand.) You have just formed your first purl-stitch. You will continue in this manner until the stitches that were on the left-hand needle have become purl-stitches on your right-hand side (n).

n

Increasing Stitches-

In many patterns, the directions will ask you to increase. To increase, you need to move the needle with the stitches back to the left-hand in order to begin the next row. Increasing stitches will allow you to shape the project that you are knitting.

Step O…When you increase, start by using the same method that you used when you were forming a knit-stitch. In fact, you will create a knit-stitch only, instead of transferring the stitch from left-hand needle onto the right, you will form another stitch behind the same stitch.

o

Step P… After two stitches have been knit into the initial stitch, you will need to slide both of these new stitches onto the right-hand needle. The picture below illustrates how the new stitches on the right-hand should look. You will create new stitches whenever your directions tell you to.

p

Decreasing Stitches-

Another way to shape your pattern is by decreasing stitches (q). To decrease stitches, you can follow one of the procedures described below. (Your instructions should tell you when to decrease and which method to use.)

Step Q...The first way to decrease stitches is by knitting two stitches together (q). You can do this by pushing your right-hand needle through two stitches at the same time, using the method that you used when knitting one stitch.

q

Step R... When you do this, the two stitches will be transferred from the left-hand to the right-hand needle as a single stitch (r).

r

Decreasing- a second method-

Step S... Another way to decrease is usually not described as decreasing. Your directions will instruct you to sl 1, k 1, and psso. Whenever the directions tell you to follow this procedure, you will understand that you are decreasing stitches by using this special method. The abbreviations mean to slip one stitch (sl 1), knit one (k 1) stitch, then psso - pass a slip stitch over the knit stitch. First you will slip one stitch onto the right-hand needle.

s

Step T... Next you will knit a stitch and move it to the right-hand needle (t).

t

Step U... Now you will insert the left-hand needle through the first loop (the slip-stitch) and you will pass this slipped-stitch over your knit-stitch (remaining on the needle) to form one stitch (u).

u

Binding off-

Step V…When you have completed a section (or all) of your project, you'll be ready to bind-off. To bind-off, you will knit or purl the first two stitches from your left hand onto the right-hand needle. At this point, you'll only have two stitches on the right-hand needle. (v)

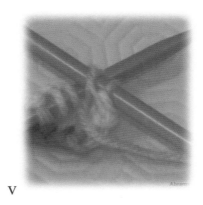

v

Step W…Next insert the tip of the left-hand needle into the front of the first stitch that was knit onto the right-hand needle. With the left-hand needle tip, slip that first stitch up and over your second stitch, on the right-hand needle. Pull gently on the yarn trying not to pull this stitch too tightly (w).

w

Step X... You will again have only one stitch on the right hand needle (the second stitch that you knit in the first pair of stitches). Now you will knit a new stitch onto the right-hand needle, so that once again you will have two stitches on the needle in your right hand. Again, slip the first stitch over the newly created second stitch. Continue the knitting one and slipping one off procedure until you have a single stitch remaining on your needle. You will then cut off an eight to ten inch length of yarn. Slip the cut end through the remaining loop. Remove the loop from the needle and securely tie-off the knot. You will leave the tail on, so that you can stitch a seam on your project, or you will cut it off and weave it invisibly into the back side of the piece. It is recommended that you tie another knot in order to secure the end (x).

x

Casting on in the middle of the row-

Step Y… Occasionally you will be required to bind-off in the middle of a project to form a button hole or another type of opening. When you do this, you will usually be required to replace the number of stitches that were initially bound-off, before continuing with your knitting.

In order to do this, you will need to cast-on stitches in the midst of the next row. Your knitting instructions will require that you replace the stitches by casting-on a certain number of stitches. You will need to take your right thumb and form a loop with your skein of yarn. (y)

y

Step Z… Next you will put the right-hand needle beneath the front of the loop that you just created with your thumb, slip the loop off the tip of your thumb onto your right-hand needle. You'll continue to follow the procedure the number of times that you have been instructed to in your directions. You should again have the original number of stitches.

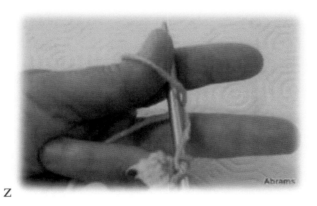

Z

NOW that you have followed Steps A-Z you are ready to begin your first project!

Five Easy Patterns

"Knitting provides me with a restful retreat from a stressful day. I love the way the colors mix… like a setting sun or a gorgeous landscape! I enjoy increasing the stitches, on at a time, to create a triangular shawl that reminds me of a beautiful water-color painting!" Tamara

To complete the following patterns, you will need between one to eight ounces of yarn (25-250 grams), depending on the project. All patterns require US size 10 needles (except for the shawl pattern which uses US size 13 straight needles). All of the patterns can be adjusted according to the gauge requirements.

Basic Headband

Yarn and Supplies

About 1 ounce of yarn
US Size 10 Straight Needles
Darning Needle and Scissors

Size: One Size (headband will stretch)
About 2 ½ inches x 21 inches (6.5 x 53 cm) - length can be adjusted to fit head size
Gauge: 10 stitches x 17 rows = about a 2 ½ x 2 ½ inch square (6.5 x 6.5 cm)

Form a slip-knot on your left-hand needle then cast on 9 more stitches (10 stitches). To begin, insert the right-hand needle tip through the knot on the left-hand needle, from front to back. Wrap the length of yarn from the skein, around the right-hand needle tip and bring the right-needle through the slip-knot, thereby creating a second loop. Slide this loop up, over, and onto the left-hand needle. Continue until all 10 stitches have been formed on the left-hand needle, to include the original knot.

Knit the next row.* Continue knitting in garter stitch until the headband is about 21 inches long. Bind off the ten stitches by knitting two stitches, lifting the first stitch over the second, then knitting another until 9 stitches have been bound off and one stitch remains. Cut off a 12-13 inch length of yarn. Thread the darning needle with the tail of yarn. Bring it through the loop, tying it off.

Stitch the two ends together by holding them together, stitching from one side to the other, securely sewing the ends together. Tie off. The remaining yarn can be woven through the edge of the headband, tied again, and cut.

Note: The headband can easily be made wider, shorter or longer. A wider band, knit from heavier yarn, will be perfect for winter weather. A smaller band with a decorative flower or ribbon attached can make a lovely gift for a little girl or for an infant.

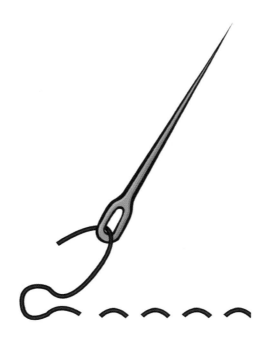

Easy Scarf with Fringe

Yarn and Supplies

About 7 ounces of yarn (200gr)
US Size 10 Straight Needles
Crochet hook (optional) and scissors

Size: One Size - about 7 ½ inches wide by 55 inches long (19 cm x 140 cm)
Gauge: 10 stitches x 17 rows = about a 2 ½ x 2 ½ inch square (6.5 x 6.5 cm)

Basic Scarf

Cast on: 30 stitches.

Knit first row*. Continue knitting each row, using a garter stitch pattern, until the scarf measures about 55 inches in length. Bind off. Tie the end and weave any loose ends of yarn into the scarf.

Fringe (Optional): Create 74 strands of yarn for each end of the scarf about 8 inches long (20 cm) long. (You may want to cut a cardboard rectangle the width of the scarf and the length of the fringe – about 7 ½ x 4 inches. You can then wrap the yarn 74 times around the cardboard, then cut along one edge of the width. This will create 74 -

8 inch lengths of fringe.) For each fringe, hold two pieces of the yarn together and fold them in half, forming a looped end and an open end. Using a medium-sized crochet hook push the hook through the first stitch at the edge of one end of the scarf. Pull the looped end of the fringe through the scarf's edge, pulling the folded-twist end through to create a loop. Now, bring the open end of each fringe through the loop (folded-twist). Pull to tighten. Continue to form 74 single or 37 double fringed pieces along each end of the scarf, then trim the ends evenly.

Variations: You can use two (or more) colors to knit a stripped scarf. Switch colors every few inches to create strips. The fringe pieces may also be doubled and more than one color can be used.

Simple Hat for Children

Yarn and Supplies

About 2.5 ounces of yarn (about 70 grams)
US Size 10 Straight Needles
Darning Needle and Scissors

Size: Child's Size (Adjust gauge as necessary.)
Gauge: 10 stitches x 17 rows = about a 2 ½ x 2 ½ inch square (6.5 x 6.5 cm)

Cast on: 68 stitches:

Row one… *k 2, p 2, repeat from *across row. Repeat row one until the ribbed-piece measures about 8 inches (20 cm).

Decrease first series…* k 2 together, p 2, repeat from * across row (51 stitches remain). On the next row * k 1, p 2, repeat from * across row, then continue k 1, p 2 ribbing for eight more rows.

Decrease second series…*k 1, p 2 together… repeat from the * across row (34 stitches remain). In the next row, *k 1, p 1, repeat from * across row, then continue in the k 1, p 1 ribbing for eight more rows.

Decrease third series… k 2 together all the way across the row (16 stitches will remain).

Decrease fourth series…p 2 together all the way across the row (8 stitches will remain). Cut the yarn and leaving a 12-16 inch tail. Thread the darning needle with this cut end, and guide it through the eight remaining stitches on the knitting needle. Draw the yarn through twice, tightening securely, then tie off the end. Stitch to create a seam.

Note: Different colors of leftover yarn can be used to make stripes. Larger needles, or an increased number of stitches, can be used to knit a hat for an adult.

Fringed Garter-Stitch Shawl

Yarn and Supplies

About 18 ounces of yarn (510 grams)
US Size 13 Straight Needles
Darning Needle and Scissors

Size: Triangular - one size fits all – about 65 inches wide x 43 inches long, (165cm x 127cm) including fringe
Gauge: 9 stitches x 17 rows = 4 inches (10 cm)

Cast on: two stitches
Row one - Knit both stitches
Row two - Knit one, yarn over (yo) (increasing one stitch), k next stitch. Continue in this manner, increasing one stitch as you begin each new row by using the same method, k-1, yo (inc 1), k til end of every row*. Repeat* until your shawl measures 36 inches from the beginning row.

Bind of loosely.

Cut fringe pieces to measure 14 inches. Fold each 14 inch piece in half and use a crochet hook (see scarf directions) to loop and pull the fringe along the side edges of your shawl

Easy Baby Blanket

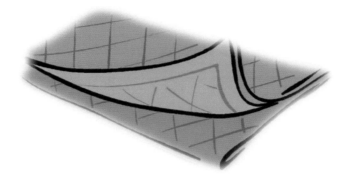

Yarn and Supplies:

Medium Weight Yarn: 7 ounces (about 200 grams)
Size 10 US Straight Needles
Size: One Size – approximately 27 ½ inches x 30 inches (70 cm x 76 cm)
Gauge: 10 stitches x 17 rows = about a 2 ½ x 2 ½ inch square (6.5 x 6.5 cm)

Cast on: 111 stitches.

1st -4th rows: Use a k 1, p 1 seed pattern across each of the rows, always starting and ending with a k stitch.

(5th row: Use a k 1, p 1, k 1, p 1, on the first four stiches, then knit across the rest of this row until you reach the last four stitches… end with p 1, k 1, p 1, and k 1.

6th row: Use a k 1, p 1, k 1, p 1 pattern on the first four stitches. Purl the remainder of row until you reach the last four stitches… end with a p 1, k 1, p 1, k1, for the last four stitches in row six.)*

*Continue to work even with the 5th and 6th row pattern for the next 29 inches (74 cm).

Last four rows: Work in the seed-stitch pattern across each of the last four rows. Bind off and weave in any loose ends.

Happy Knitting!

"I take my knitting with me everywhere I go. It's the perfect pastime when I'm traveling or visiting with friends. Even though I've been knitting for years, I enjoy simple patterns that allow me to experience what is going on around me." Anna

Learning to knit is an ongoing process. While it may be frustrating at times, the long-term results are certain to bring you hours of pleasure, to say nothing of the excitement your friends and family will experience when you present them with lovely hand-knit gifts!

The best advice is to relax and enjoy! Knitting is a cherished, old-fashioned tradition that is certain to bring you hours of gratification and lasting satisfaction!

"Knitting, a timeless hobby, a rainy day craft, a way to tie fringe to shawl, mind to heart, generation to generation…" Jessica

Printed in Great Britain
by Amazon